I HAVE CONFUSED A FIST FOR A FLAG.

IT WAS A NAVIGATIONAL ERROR,

A COLLUSION OF CORAL AND FIBERGLASS.

WINNER OF THE 2015
SAWTOOTH POETRY PRIZE

ED ROBERSON, JUDGE

AHSAHTA PRESS
BOISE, IDAHO

STEREO.
ISLAND.
MOSAIC.

VINCENT TORO

Ahsahta Press, Boise State University, Boise, Idaho 83725-1525

Cover design by Quemadura / Book design by Janet Holmes

ahsahtapress.org

LIBRARY OF CONGRESS CATALOGING-IN-PUBLICATION DATA

Names: Toro, Vincent, 1975- author.

Title: Stereo. Island. Mosaic. / Vincent Toro.

Description: Boise, Idaho : Ahsahta Press, 2016. | Series: Sawtooth Poetry Prize ; 2015

Identifiers: LCCN 2015049413| ISBN 9781934103654 (pbk. : alk. paper) | ISBN 1934103659 (pbk. : alk. paper)

Classification: LCC PS3620.O5878 A6 2016 | DDC 811/.6—dc23

LC record available at http://lccn.loc.gov/2015049413

FOR GRISEL

ACKNOWLEDGMENTS AND THANKS

I offer my most sincere thanks to the editors of the following literary journals and sites for being the first to publish the following poems: *The Acentos Review*: "Cabo Rojo Fresco" and "Operation Bootstrap (Right Panel)" (under the title "The Inscrutable Art of Bootstrapping"); *Border-senses*: "Metastasis"; *The Buenos Aires Review*: "Crab Canon for the Marooned" (under the title "Recursion Sonata for Piano and Feather Duster"), "Crepuscule with Grisel" (under the title "a whisper. a squeeze. a trembling."), "Fibonacci Ekphrastic for 'Birth of City' by Angel Rodriguez-Diaz," "Operation Commonwealth" (under the title "the world has accused you"),"Sorta Rican Book of Dreams (Abridged Version)"; *The Caribbean Writer*: "Sucrosanct"; *The Cortland Review*: "Alzheimer's Suite (for Sammy)"; *Duende*: "Threnody for Jim Just Jim"; *The Journal*: "Exoskeletons, or the Secret Life of a Stargazer"; *The Journal of American Studies Turkey*: "Decímarinas"; *Kweli*: "Guanín"; *The Ostrich Review*: "Grito: An Alternate History of the Parranda"; *The Poet's House*: "Rumsong" (under the title "Captain Morgan"); *Vinyl*: "Heliotropic Crab Canon."

Because it takes a nation of millions to raise a book (and its author) I must send my most ardent thanks to the following people and organizations: Dr. Grisel Y. Acosta. My punk poet profesora, mi vida, you must come before all others and have your own lines here, for you have no equal. *Familia*: My parents, Kathy and Felix Toro. Carmen Rivera and Candido Tirado (for first calling me "poet"). Rev. Samuel and Yolanda Acosta. Vivian and Paul Simon. Juana Carrera-Lipsky. The Riveras of Borinquen (Mercedes, Mario Jr., Yelly, & co.), in whose home some of this book was written. *Organizations/Institutions*: Ahsahta Press. The Rutgers University Creative Writing Program. The Geraldine R. Dodge Poetry Foundation. The Poet's House. The New York Foundation for the Arts. The Dreamyard Project. The Cooper Union Saturday Program. The Macondo Foundation. The Guadalupe Cultural Arts Center. Gemini Ink. Can Serrat Artist Retreat. *Mentors/Collaborators/Samaritans/Editorial and Emotional Support*: Janet Holmes. Ed Roberson. Pedro Pietri. Miguel Algarin. Saul Williams. Rigoberto Gonzalez. John Keene. Alice Elliott Dark. Rachel Hadas. Kristin Prevallet. Willie Perdomo. Cornelius Eady. Wayne Koestenbaum. Naomi Shihab Nye. Dr. Norma Cantu. Wendy Barker. Ruth Behar. Marjorie Agosin. Ching-In Chen. Linda Rodriguez. Ellen Placey Wadey. J. Michael Martinez. Jim and Lucia LaVilla-Havelin. Pedro Ramirez. Charles Fambro. Marina Gutierrez. Tim Lord. Jason Duchin. Ellen Hagan and David Flores. John Ellrodt. Maria Fico. Jim Haba. Martin Farawell. Khalil Murrell. Ruben Quesada. Eduardo Corral. Francisco Aragon. Michael Van Calbergh. *Amigos*: Andrew DiClemente. Gerrard Briones. Terence Simon. Thaxton Lewis. Jim Anderson (1975–1996). Jeff Romstedt. Steven Serrano. Alex Khost. Derek Beres. Antowand Harris. Nick Merchant. Nova Gutierrez. Greg Segarra. Bobby DeJesus. Joe Doeffinger. And many thanks to all my students in New York, New Jersey, Texas, and Turkey. You've all taught me more than I could possibly ever teach you.

CONTENTS

ISLAND: PALENQUES

MOSAIC: ZEMÍS

MOSAIC: ZEMÍS

Employing a single channel of transmission, the monophonic player emits a sound from a definite origin. The stereophonic player, on the other hand, employs two channels and disperses the sound so that it reaches the listener seemingly from everywhere and nowhere. The voice emerging from the stereo, like the voice emerging from the hybridized subject, becomes an uncertain presence by having no singular point of reference. In this way, the hybrid becomes not merely a dual-consciousness, but "less than one and double" and "almost but not quite." It also becomes that which generates paranoia on the part of the listener who hears something from an unstable source, for "in that other scene of colonial power, where history turns to farce and presence to 'a part,' can be seen the twin figures of narcissism and paranoia that repeat furiously, uncontrollably," and this paranoia in turn reinforces the marginalization of the minority, the deterritorialization of the hybrid, the deterritorialization that then reinforces the hybrid as hybrid in a closed cycle.

—Sandy Florian, *The Hybrid*

Zemís are divine objects in the Taino culture. Often, but not exclusively, made from stone or fabric, the Zemís were perceived as keys to the spirit world, material representations of the unseen. They were also created as memorials to those who had passed on into the spirit world or to major events that occurred in the tribe's history.

Bootstrap:

1. *v.* To help oneself. To not rely on another or ask for a handout. To toughen up and deal with the problem on your own. To know there is no one to depend on. You got to do it yourself, pull yourself up by your own bootstraps, as they say.

2. *v.* To remodel a Caribbean island into an industry. To convert jibaros into assembly line products. To break in a horse. To potty train the landscape. To vaccinate. To anesthetize. To repackage a population. To eradicate autonomy, force feeding a codependence on foreign economies through deletion of ecology and language.
    —*Also see Operation Bootstrap, Puerto Rico, 1954–Present*

3. *v.* To devise a complex computer system from a simple set of coded symbols. To create a vast universe from a mere handful of raw materials. To be crafty and resourceful. To create a new language from the remnants of an obsolete one. To make a whole lot of something out of nothing, like using 36 chromosomes to build a man.

4. *v.* To use the master's table scraps to expand these quarters. To undo the done by applying twenty-six letters or less. To make one remark to spark revelation. To conduct reconstructive surgery with a butter knife. To freeze the flow of access to the entire eastern seaboard from a secondhand laptop. To turn two coconuts into a short wave radio, like turning sand and rocks into a cosmopolis. To commit sorcery. To use two sticks to ignite the flame for feast.

EXOSKELETONS, OR THE SECRET LIFE OF A STARGAZER

When father's belt drummed up green
     and pink blots that spread across his ass
and thigh like a map of the Tau Ceti system,
     the boy fantasized about a race

of Martians possessing exoskeletons,
     and he wished that he might have been
born bone above flesh with an organic suit
     of armor to guard him. When knuckles

struck the boy's cheek, inexplicable questions
     about the cosmos arose from each blow,
provoking him to recall the difference between
     Red Dwarfs and White Dwarfs. The sting

of Mother's stiletto on his ribs dissolved
     like an asteroid piercing the nebulous
surface of Jupiter. As the space between
     her knee and his stomach decreased

at high velocity he became closer to things
     distant. Astronomy became his anodyne.
He declared that he would apply his mind
     to calculating the chance of life in other

solar systems. Junior stargazers would study
     his lectures proposing the coming
of a civilization consisting entirely of gaseous
     particles, entities that had no need

for an unreliable sack of soft tissue. Each kick
     conjured visions of extra-terrestrials
unburdened by marrow or shell. Every slap
     left him imagining a species that made

love by exchanging codes of silver and orange
    beams of light, creatures lacking a solid
frame who could therefore do no harm to one
    another with whip or steel or tongue.

THE ROADS OF BORINQUEN

snake like Igneris plodding down
                the Toro Verde mountains.
They shake and shimmy like Giovanni Hidalgo's
            palms, like palm trees
cambered from sand to sky.
                    They juke jive like wild

bougainvilleas splintering into rain
                  forests of cell towers.
              They reach into salt flats and twirl
                    up into Sunday
worship at the sprawling lechoneras of Guavate.
           The roads of Borinquen slope

           and careen like guayaba trees caught
              in the crosswind, like the dirt
terraces of Yauco sprouting coffee beans,
                or the dust of our misguided
slang that Esmerelda sweeps
            from the patio. They taper

                and they bloat like arteries
        pumping sun into the canciones
that feed us, swaying like hammocks
              slung across mango trees
where first kisses seed into copper saints.
          The roads of Borinquen shape

shift like domino tables once midday
      strikes. They contort
        like town criers, slide like razor
blades over four-day-old beards,
                 or the machete blade
through the caña that mysteriously makes its way

onto our mesas. The roads of Borinquen
                              veer from the promise
            of the Caciques to the promise of two
                        for one quarter pounders
      and back again like a waterfall
of zemís cascading into a landscape

            of rental cars parked on bateys. They curve
and jump like cockfights through
                        colonial plazas littered with juggling
      pajaritos, roller blades, and angelic vagrants
                  as if trying to shake free from the surf
                              shops and department

      stores like a pair of dusty chancletas.
The roads of Borinquen wind dive
                              upward into the arms
            of the Virgins on every wall in every
                        casita in the hillside.
They blindside like sparring partners in the gym

            behind the old sugar mill. The roads of Borinquen
                              burrow through cities
named after slain warriors: —Jayuya, Cayey, Utuado—
                  as if to pour salt on wounds
            beyond healing. They lull like Lilliana who still
laments surrendering the mountains

                        for the city. They sing and surprise
like the neighbors springing up
                  on doorsteps at three in the morning
armed with guidos and warm rum
                        screaming *bomba!*
      before carrying us gently

                        back to bed, cradling us as we
            dream. The roads of Borinquen stretch
                        like sunbathing cobwebs. They pull pranks
in the form of covert potholes and cow
                        crossings, then invite us
            to Joyuda for steamed langosta.

The roads of Borinquen steer into the gulleys
                        where the ancestors have buried
                        the villages secrets.
            They swoop up into the moon
            that each night promises us a chance
to become the myths our masters spill into the sea.

FIBONACCI EKPHRASTIC FOR "THE BIRTH OF A CITY" BY ANGEL RODRIGUEZ-DIAZ

Your

map

is made

of burnt leaves

and woodpecker wings.

Decades levitate the counters

you scrubbed. Echinacea engraved across your breast grows

without roots to bind them. You breathe unwashed linens, never ask for keys to the convent.

Your

map

is scaled

down to match

your expectations.

Expelled from the geometry

of myth, rumor becomes crown and mask. You beautify

chicken wire and cracked drywall with heirlooms from Aztlan. What you possess you have reared.

Your

map

is strewn

with letters

home, dried apricots,

dented pickups, and tired men

who work too long and drink too hard. Cedar ash congests

the lungs you use to blow out virgin candles bought at the neighborhood botanica.

Your

map

is marred

by borders

that become a sieve

of history, straining the wild

from the willing. Missions and malls encroach your sun swathed

villitas where flowers battle and murals proliferate like thirsty brushfires.

THRENODY FOR JIM JUST JIM

If I have a gift to offer in return, It is always a poem.
—James Anderson (6/20/1975–10/8/1996)

You as the grass growing wings that are you, as halogen
lamp dimming in the window of a 5th-floor walk up,
as wise epitaph wedged in white marble, as eloquent
tourniquet, as an egg and cheese sandwich in a Turnpike
diner. You as rich mendicant in a green button down

> *Are you leaving? Yep. Where are you going? Sisters.*

sweater. You as starving alley cat brushing bare heels, as bidi
trapped in your chapped lemon peel lips, as Birkenstocks
smearing monochrome Twomblys across kitchen floors,
as leather coat you gave to a homeless man freezing
on Manhattan sidewalks. You as emperor of ice cream

> *Are you leaving? Yep. Where are you going? Sisters.*

and green tea. You as the hard words we flee
like airborne toxins, as a yellow jacket self-extracting
its stinger, as broken bones and scratched corneas,
as sarcophagus of faded album covers and rusty woks.
You as general in the war on insincerity. You as canvas

> *Are you leaving? Yep. Where are you going? Sisters.*

of scabs I wear around my wrist, as a plastic ash tray,
as an Andean mountain made of secondhand books,
as illusory deer dodging your '88 Mazda, as lead zephyr,
as tragic epilogue, as omitted poet. You as the patron
saint of cracked spirits and cracked dashboards. You

Are you leaving? Yep. Where are you going? Sisters.
Are you leaving? Yep. Where are you going? Sisters.
Are you leaving? Yep. Where are you going? Sisters.

as Jim Just Jim.

SORTA RICAN BOOK OF DREAMS (ABRIDGED VERSION)

Computer

1. With human hands that pokes you when you try to type
   means you will forgive yourself for a mistake you never
   had the sense to make.
2. Singing to you like Hector Lavoe means that your oldest
   daughter will grow up to become the director of shrubbery
   at a bankrupt amusement park.

Ladybug

1. Crawling on the hood of your car means you will inherit
   a vast collection of incomplete maps.
2. Swimming in a bowl of soup means you will forget your
   wife's birthday after you forget that you never married.

Mango

1. Eating one while a chimpanzee folds your laundry means
   the IRS will mistakenly pronounce you dead and offer your
   mother a tax refund they'll ask her to return.
2. One with feet that chases you through a botanica means
   that your wardrobe is outdated.

Pie

1. Gigantic blueberry pies that randomly disappear and reappear
   means that a building will be renovated on the south side
   of your block.
2. A pear pie left out in the middle of a superhighway means
   a dead relative wants back the bottle of Presidente
   they gave you last Christmas.

ALZHEIMER'S SUITE (FOR SAMMY)

1.

Still dons his Guayabera at church. Still scuttles
across rooms reprising the soccer matches of his youth
in Barranquilla. Still hears his mother declaring, "In this house
we are ruled by only education and God." Still sings his favorite
Cumbias as he waters the garden. Still mourns his great
aunt killed by her alcoholic husband. Still giggles
with his wife as they watch Cantinflas confound
his foe with nonsense discourse. Still holds a grudge
against the winter wind of Lake Michigan. Still prays
at every meal, promising to turn its energy
into love. Still smitten with the scent of aguacate, the taste
of butter pecan. Still hides for his grandchildren to seek him.

2.

Still   his   church   scuttles
        rooms   r   ising   his youth
            a quill . Still he   is   other   cl ing   his house
                led by   an   ill   his favorite
Cumbias   a   garden   urn is
            killed by   alcohol   . Still giggles
With   wife   he   Can   confound
his   nonsense   course. Still
            the winter wind   an   ill prays
At every meal,   sing to turn
into   smitten   aguacate, he
                can   till   his   children   see him.

13

3.
Still   scuttles
              rooms   in   s outh
        a quill Still   other   ing   his   use
                                                               ill   is   a rite

        bias   a   den
              killed by   a co ol   Still giggles
                     if   he   Can   con
                     nonsense   . Still
                     inter wind   ill rays
At eve   sing to
                     smit e   agua
                     an   ill   chi de   s him.

4.
Still

              ill   ill

                                                            ill

        illed   ill

                          . Still
                                                  ill

                     ill   .

5.

ISLAND: PALENQUES

Palenques are cities that were founded by runaway slaves. They were also commonly known as quilombos.

TAÍNOBELISK

South

During
the festival
of La Noche
de San Juan
Yuisa dives
into the tide
at Naguabo,
shucking sins
like corn husks.
A murky undertow
seizes her.
She surrenders
to its pull,
resurfaces four
centuries later
at Orchard Beach.

North

.

Now lost on
City Island,
Yuisa searches
for herself beneath
rusty spring
mattresses,
in Irish pubs
and at the
Botanical
gardens.
The laughter
of children
converges.
A bridge is
constructed under
a bridge of sky.

THE BLOCK, ROMARE BEARDEN, 1972

439 Lenox

Diabetic tenement torso.
Liquor store took Orishas
on disability hostage.
5th Floor hangover. Kids
make mousetrap Play
Stations. A traffic jelly.
Acrylic skyline reduced
to smudged spectacles.

441 Lenox

Bare pall bearers boost
WWII vet from 7D. Made
his last Con Ed Payment.
Leopard skin lady sobs.
Carrot cake and tall tales
served up in Sunday best.
From busted fire escapes
orange cherubim descend.

443 Lenox

Earl Hines legato subdued
by the barking of Manny
from 6H out on the curb,
begging Irma to let him back
in after she changed the locks
because he let OTB take
the rent. He calls, but no
response. Call and Recall.

445 Lenox

Blue Roses bleed around
neck of the Sunrise Baptist.
A neon light emits myths:
Ellison, Robeson, Baldwin.
School is held on Tio's knee.
Week's bochinche squawks
heavy like old testament,
curt like AM news radio.

447 Lenox

Making love's eviction
notice urgent. Defunct
fireplaces. Hopping roof
tops in scuffed Hi-tops.
Dull dagger nostrils seek
refuge in the VFW. Bum
sages rise from grates, seek
symmetry in brown brick.

449 Lenox

The owner of the Mirror
Barbershop was Professor
of Physics in Sudan. Shaves
come with free lessons
on the Unified Field Theory.
A makeshift octet mounts
the pigeonsills, blurts purple
prayers to oily Orisha vista.

DÉCIMARINA

San Juan, 2010

Fortuño strokes his tie, cocksure,
simpers at the camera crew,
bloviates, then kneels at his pew
before ordering the seizure
of the college. Suits of azure
sweep the campus with pepper spray
and boot heels, a pill to allay
both student umbrage and the fears
of tourists and lenders. Veneers
patched. Luis jettisoned. With pay.

The décima is a poetry and song form invented by Vicente Espinel during the late 1500s. It is a ten-line stanza consisting of octosyllabic lines with a rhyme scheme of ABBAACCDDC. The subject matter of the poems is often philosophical, religious, lyrical, or political in nature. As songs, they are often improvised, and as a result, the eight-syllable line requirement is a loose one. Some lines may be seven or nine syllables long. The form survives today most prominently as the structure of the Puerto Rican musical style known as the Plena.

CRAB CANON FOR THE MAROONED

Pink water above,
            black sky recedes into
    tilted highways and crimeless alibis.
                Charred fingers prod at stain glass eyes
confusing machine language for serenades.
    Brokers and dealers wander inside
                        their own heads and disappear, hire
        bargain basement seers to reveal
colors undiscovered. Illiterate scholars parade around
                circus tents of obscure
                        facts made obsolete by
                fiction addicts. Children rear
    their parents to become a bazaar of scuffed
            mirrors hiding from
                the scrutiny of other mirrors.
                    They are
                protected
                        Once they declare themselves
            defenseless, defenseless
                        Once they declare themselves
                protected.
                    They are
                the scrutiny of other mirrors,
            mirrors hiding from
    their parents to become a bazaar of scuffed
                fiction addicts. Children rear
                    facts made obsolete by
                circus tents of obscure
colors undiscovered. Illiterate scholars parade around
        bargain basement seers to reveal
                        their own heads and disappear, hire
    Brokers and dealers to wander inside
    confusing machine language for serenades
                    charred. Fingers prod at stain glass eyes,
        tilted highways, and crimeless alibis.
            Black sky recedes into
pink water above.

RICANSTRUCTION: DECASIA

oceanic

speech And

seaweed
sail

a Return to

Each

origin

imaginary   mosquitos   quick

to   *annex*

History

that washes up on the shoreline.
because I was

the savage   they agreed to

become for me an atoll
a joke
of monolingualism.
the fortress   refashioned
into   the rooster
squeals   .

a lost
timbale   haunted by

George Washington
graffiti laden

trash

naturalized,

rifles   confused   for
               coral   I am the
     navigational error
                            . My

     parents were

 buoys

         that
            launched themselves into

              the ribs of
                    taxable items
       Ostinoids
                ignoring the bright

unreachable quasars   on my own shoreline
     . I cooked
                    the island
   on
       light bulbs in the projects
                    .
       my citizenship

     decapitated

        by
a   biohacked   baker
    .   Rimbaud's

skull

is a

telescope,   a child

on the moon

breakdancing

a filthy

fishing wire

in the cathedral   , a   chalice

of

shoes,   His face

a   flame

for   500 years

, now

the coast

must confiscate my

bottle of rum.

blackened lungs,

cockfights

yucca And

fried pork, succulent

America?

tomes

moulded from

deep

-sea unnamabilities.   dumped

onto my scalp

toxic molasses

A sovereignty

where

women

were born faceless.

I

reattach

The

famines   of

a fisherman and a scholar

to antideluvian

contraband

wounds of

troubadours in

in Perth

Amboy   .   a house

of imprecations

burnt

, blasting

oceans   like amps

I feel

heavier.

SELF-PORTRAIT AS COFFEE TREE

It is never one's ambition to end like this—pulverized,
diluted—the baldest molecules of your being denuded
                        and dragged like an obstinate
carcass through a holiday parade.

Can you even fathom the leagues between this counter
top and the plateaus that sprouted me?

Not long ago I ached to be something more
than to be nipped with the morning's
distillation of yellow journalism.
I once had emperors pining for my scent. Legions
carted themselves across implausible parallels
to uproot me and barter me for jewels.

Noblemen annointed me as Patron Saint
of the Incontinent, to be served only during sacrament,
            the prize of every apothecary's cupboard.

Buried lonesome in the island of Martinique,
I became my own nation of millions in just half
a century. I was berries, the companion
                    of chess, until the soused took
        up with me, made me their panacea.
Soon bluenoses cast me as the bitter
invention of the devil,   Imams forbade me
                                to occupy the dining table.

I never meant to be the cause for desolation
of loamy regions,
        to become a chain for clawing moguls,
drenched in a sugary mulch for those scratching
their way across the other side of the factory whistle.

Somewhere in these tropics there is a stretch

of soil that remembers me as the musk
             that once gave the birds
        both flight and song.

If the only way back to my Oromo throne is through
your lower intestines, I am ready
                 to descend, to dive . . .

CABO ROJO FRESCO

Panorama of lush hammocks, rocking
　　　chairs mingling with untamed Flamboyans.
Maybe a radio dispatching static, an accent

of claves and splintered oxcarts combed over
　　　with weeds. Maybe sticks sprout from patches
in the backyard to mark where the caña has been

buried. El faro chaperones the salt flats. Stillness
　　　reigns over the cove. There is motion only
when a glass runs empty, a bladder is full, a fishing

rod twitches. The air is syrup poured over bronze skin.
　　　Maybe a scruffy Labrador paws innocuously
at the sand. The hills call the shots. They remain

unmentioned, maybe like a Chagall unfinished. Time
　　　is given to strangers with an ambiguous smirk.
Viejitos in the bar bark about lost loves and lost

cock fights, recite speeches from Albizu about unfair
　　　trades with uninvited guests. Half heard cantos
are pinched like a half smoked cigar and stuffed

into the pocket of a tattered guayabera. There
　　　is a hole in the roof left by the last hurricane
leaking new trends from the north onto casita

floors. Casinos cramp the horizon like a gordito
　　　on a crowded bus. A desperate breeze dries
the towel dangling from a vacant beach chair.

The natives sleep suspiciously, dreamless
　　　as the algae glows below them. A jet ski slices
the bay where carrucho is mustered for tonight's

mofongo. Mangos plummet like illusions
　　　　from the kinky hair of a schoolboy whose
sandlot has just been replaced by a strip mall.

STEREO: AREYTOS

The Areyto is a ritual performance that was conducted by the Taino Indians. These performances merged poetry, song, chanting, and dance. Both instructional tool and general entertainment, contents of the Areyto consisted of historical narratives, myths and folklore, prophecies, religious oration, and cautionary tales. The areytos were the embodiment of the epic memory and collective soul of the tribe.

OPERATION COMMONWEALTH (LEFT PANEL)

After Nicanor Parra

A circular path is carved through your front yard.
                    Pink sinkholes gather in your medicine
cabinet. You exalt busted blenders like sophisms
                              scrawled by retired scholars.
        Your life has become a shy puzzle,
                                        a canyon of foreclosures,
                    an abandoned fish market.

The world has accused you of not being a world,
                    of loving meaningless songs,
and you have responded by raising your children to unravel
                              spools of red tape across cities of wax.
        The promise of a guilt free purchase
                                        congeals like gum
                    beneath a wooden school desk.

The world has accused you of not being a world.
                    You retort with an acceptance speech
scripted by beautiful gangsters.   You live under
                              the thumb of contracts hoisted
        like minarets. Landslides court you
                                        with a hospice of deserted
                    checkout counters and comic strip altars.

Your lungs constrict in the presence of cedar and ash.
                    The world has accused you of not being
a world and you respond by offering your guests
                              sliced cheese and snow globes.
        You prod them about their holiday plans.
                                        Your path is littered
                    with toll booths and subpoenas.

You dig shallow trenches around the kitchen table.
                    Sub-contractors install a wall of plaster
teeth in your bathtub. The sea has divorced you
                              and taken the dog. The world
          has accused you of not being a world,
                                        of unhearing the voices
                    that hold together the seams

of your jacket, and you have responded
                    with despondent sighs, the kind of sigh
that makes orphans of widows.
                    Soon enough you will inherit
          the pollen of a thousand uprooted gardenias
                                        as you wait for the sunlight
                    to learn your nickname.

DÉCIMARINA

Queens, 1955

Cast from the hillsides. Shipped as freight
from one isla to another.
Swiped like orphans from their mothers.
The promise of work hung like bait.
La Guardia became the gate
offering you a safe return
once you've torn your tendons to earn
the fare back. Your plot is re-soiled.
Few will rise from out of the coiled
snakes throat to reclaim their sunburns.

SUCROSANCT

There was a time when Efrain's merengue could inspire the band
to play an extra set. When he danced it was a moon landing.

On the mound he was a sniper. His splitfinger over the inside
of the plate was a left hook launched by Willie Benitez. Pero

now Efrain has poor vision. During the last surgery they removed
half of his left foot. His hand carved walking cane is no longer

just a smooth fashion accessory. He thought he had done right by his
mother, wife, and children by keeping away from the aguardiente

and other women. The preacher never said that pasteles were a sin.
But Efrain is a Bermuda triangle for anything baked with refined sugar.

In 1871 his great grandfather's slaves torched the trapiche on his finca.
They tired of sacrificing the minutes of their lives to King Sugar.

King Sugar had driven Efrain's great grandfather insane, enticing
him to squeeze every last drop of sweat and blood and bile

from his fellow man, to bind them to the fields with charters penned
on the other side of the Atlantic. Once the slaves made a funeral

pyre of the harvest they retreated to the coasts in the hopes of paying
black market traders to sneak them off this tropical penitentiary. But

before leaving they buried the rotten teeth of a goat beneath
the big house, a ceremony to curse all descendants of the family

that cuffed them to the cane. *May their blood be corroded*
by the sugar that built their empire like termites consuming a log

cabin. May the sugar crack their marrows like the zafra broke
the backs of our children. May the sugar become the ghosts

that haunt the hallways and closets of their haciendas.
Efrain does not know that the sucrose that stole his eyes

was stillborn from the lash his great grandfather cracked
across the shoulder of every campesino who took their time

reaping his cane, that the ads for Pepsi and Coke on every
corner in his neighborhood were ghostwritten by those

who died on his family estate skinning cane stalks until
blisters arose through nautical dusk, all so his great

grandmother could fill her closet with dresses
made out of handwoven vicuña.

Prelude: Casa Grande/Prayer of the Finca

      Grant the bloodless father
this panoply of blistered
              palms, a brigade of bent
        machetes to raze this plot.
They will draw sap from every
        suckling reared inside his stable.

      There is a single
puckering mouth
            that spans the distance
        of a continent
that yawls and kicks
        when denied a lick of the lollipop.

        The dance will have to be
postponed. Today all
                        must forego the guitar
for the plow. Our bloodless
                father needs every disembodied
fabric stitched and hung.

        The cimarrones have all
been caught. The horses have been
                        saddled. The time
has come to empty every
                lung, crack the whip and stalk,
drench the island in molasses.

RUMSONG

Belly bronzed bikini wasteland
      of jello buck shots,
keg stands, and nights
      that last three days.
Jacuzzi swirl of spray tanned
      glam, the gleam of soaked
shirts and vomit as the spring
      breakers bump stumps
bury plastic pints in sand, littering
      the boardwalk with pizza
grease. They lift their middle
      fingers to the sun, flash
their cameras tops and gold
      cards, a slick arrhythmia
bobbing to the monotone
      of bass heavy dance
anthems, funneling down
      their throats gallons
of distilled cane, venerating glass
      bottles bearing the name of Captain

                  Morgan was a sunburnt cyclone,
           famous for plundering Panama
               and for cutting off clean any
           finger with a gold ring on it. He could
               empty a bohio faster than
           a tsunami, making sport of torturing
               slaves and puncturing their
           women. Morgan took pleasure in hacking
               off the limbs of village children
           while those he shackled were mining
               for his gold. These deeds earned
           him knighthood from the English crown
               They say before his death
           he gutted three of his men so they could

guard his treasure in the afterlife,
and that today he still sails the Atlantic
as a phantasm, chasing down
the descendents of his enemies,
snuffing them in their   dreams
by drowning them in rum.

TO GOVERNOR PEZUELA, ON BANNING THE MERENGUE

In 1849 Juan De La Pezuela, Puerto Rico's Governor, appointed by Spain, declared an official prohibition on the merengue. During this time a person could be fined for allowing it to be danced in their homes, and someone caught dancing the merengue could serve up to ten days in prison.

You trounced upon our palm
      leaf castles and we did not

wince. We obliged. You demanded all
      tribesmen beyond the age

of fifteen cloak themselves and speak
      in your serrated patois. We obliged.

You browbeat us to abandon our fishing
      nets and take up your machetes

and your plow. We obliged. We obliged
      you when you compelled us

to round up our gods who massaged
      our shoulders callously knotted

by the trapiche. At your command we
      placed them in a birdcage and hung

them at the entrance of your hacienda,
      only to watch you drown them

in the bay. Now you pass a law to deafen
      our footsteps, to keep us still, muted

through the destitute night in an effort
      to ration our sweat for the harvest

This time, we promise that you will have
　　　　better luck begging the coquis

to keep hush. For you may lay claim
　　　　to our days, our blood may

appear to cascade solely to fill your
　　　　reservoir, but no law you scribe

can keep reefs from bending to tidal
　　　　shifts or arms from linking

like a balustrade, our physiques
　　　　billowing electric with gusts

of guitar and hand claps, churning spiral
　　　　galaxies across hillsides

with a 1,2 . . . 1,2,3 . . . 1,2 . . . 1,2,3 . . .
　　　　From your den you can see

across the river a bonfire flirting
　　　　with starlight, can hear the pulse

of drums and serfs eloping, unabashed
　　　　and incorrigible, and you

swelling with arrhythmia, offended
　　　　by our will to keep time.

SUGAR ISLAND FUGUE

First Voice: 1521

When smallpox struck down
        nearly every native
the encomenderos were left
        with no esclavos
to work in the mines.

They turned to sugar
        as their mode of plunder,
planting thousands of acres
        of cane from the beach
to the mountains.

But they overestimated
        what profit might spring
when they underestimated
        the ants who were
true lords of this land.

The ants devoured the candied
        tableau, consuming
every stalk like a brush fire
        let loose, doing
to the crops what the encomenderos

did to the farmers. They called
        on their saints to stop
the swarm, though some thought
        it might have been
the saints that sent the ants.

The saints never arrived to help
        extinguish the ants,
because even saints know there

is no force that can stop
tiny hungry things once they

catch scent of something sweet.

MYTHOPOEIA

After Brathwaite and Walcott

Spear Sundial Compass Totem fastened to soil, remnant
artifact denoting demise of those dressed in pulp of cane
stalks, unmoored lithe and sunsculpted who swamdanced

through humid musk where the only exchange was a fair one:
three goats for a tale and three buckets of wheat. Foliage grew
from rainbows, meticulous mellow librettos of copper

citizens caught in a contradanza of sea and smoke. The last
hurricane lugged wood fish ashore, platoons of pale zombies
who uprooted the crops. Land became merely a surface,

as their suits were merely a surface. The village now merely
a resource to pillage. The survivors of the plague fled
to the peak of El Yunque where they hid in the hills for ten

generations. Each month they sent a scout crawling through
the cracks past prisons and missions into the abyss to gather
provisions. Last time the sojourn was taken the scout stumbled

upon a bottle cap, mistook it for a zemí, returned to camp
carrying the mysterious sphere, buried the tin disk
at the perimeter of their refuge. Six days later a visitor dressed

sheep's wool arrived wielding an obsidian scepter and a scroll
bound in pig's hide. The stranger spoke lilted gibberish, ate
provisions of guava and qenepas offered by the village's children.

This well tailored phantasm scratched marks onto pressed leaf,
rerouting the tribe's trajectory with the slash of a feather dipped
in oil. The uninvited guest uprooted the spear that guarded

their presence, aimed his scepter cloudward, conjuring thunder, and with an unsettling grin drawn across his face he casually exited the scene. The following morning half of the women

in the village did not wake up and every elder had vanished. By mid-afternoon the tribe's entire harvest had died. By nightfall a green gurgling grew from below.

EPICENTER:
CARIBBEAN SEA CRAB CANON

EBB TIDE

Sea swallowed by beckoning ship.

     Cargo of people hoisted from decks

like cracked masts.   Sand city

     sacked by circus of preening prawns.

Griots punish them with silence.

     The cook casts old tires upon rapids

and descends into waterfall euphoria.

     Cimarrones emerge as oysters,

as barnacles clutching the hull

     of time.   Few will blossom

into buoys bouncing above storms

     until heat stroke hallucinations

pull them ashore.   All crawl

     valiantly toward myth of palenques.

HURACÁN

as valiantly   of
     will sea
          preening
stroke hull   blossom
     Storms of
swallowed   casts
into and   ashore
     euphoria them
          from   until
emerge   punish like
     tires barnacles
descend   old into of of
     circus pull
with   clutching above
cimarrons waterfall
     hoisted
     oysters
     toward
     hallucinations
by as beckoning   the all
     myth
     cracked   rapids
     palenques them
     time ship by   few
upon prawns   masts   people
     silence
     bouncing
crawl
     decks buoys
     cargo   griots

MEIOSIS

Storms of silence
                    emerge
          pull hull
                         into heat
               cook euphoria like prawns

beckoning sand people
                    clutching barnacles

          of time

sacked palenques   valiantly

          blossom   as sea of cargo
               above cracked city

               old griots
                    descend from cimarrons
into waterfall

by bouncing toward myth
                    as preening oysters

          few crawl with masts hoisted

                         the ship will punish
them by stroke
                         of rapids
               upon swallowed decks

          the circus tires
buoys them   and casts
          ashore
                         all hallucinations
until

FLOW TIDE

Until hallucinations,   all ashore casts

               and them buoys.   Tires circus.

Decks swallowed upon rapids of stroke,

               by them punish,   will ship

the hoisted masts with crawl.
                         Few oysters

               preening as myth toward

bouncing, by waterfall into cimarrons from

               descends griots.   Old city
                         cracked

about cargo of sea,   as blossom valiantly.

Palenques sacked time of barnacles,

               clutching people.   Sand
                         beckoning

prawns like euphoria.   Cook heat into hull.

          The pull.

Emerge   silence of storms.

52

STEREO: AREYTOS

The culture of the Caribbean, at least in its most distinctive aspect, is not terrestrial but aquatic, a sinuous culture where time unfolds irregularly and resists being captured by the cycles of clock and calendar. The Caribbean is the natural and indispensible realm of marine currents, of waves, of folds and double folds, of fluidity and sinuosity. It is, in the final analysis, a culture of the meta-archipelago: a chaos that returns, a detour without purpose, a continual flow of paradoxes; it is a feedback machine with asymmetrical workings, like the sea, the wind, the clouds, the uncanny novel, the food chain, the music of Malaya, Gödel's theorem and fractal mathematics.

—Antonio Benitez-Rojo, *The Repeating Island*

TAÍNOBELISK

West

Yuisa plays
basketball
on a court
of broken glass.
Saudade spreads
like Starbucks
through
the East Side. Star
struck citizens
purchase flowers
from a floating
bodegua, watch
boredom like
Kung Fu films
on a Saturday
afternoon.

East

Yuisa discovers
a conch shell
on the Brooklyn-
bound D train.
She holds it
up to her
ear and hears
a jazz quartet,
Dolphin speak,
A kitten
pawing at steel
doors.
Congueros
disappear
and reappear
at each station.

DÉCIMARINA

Rincon, 1771

Don Rincon was appointed heir
to his master's plush plantation
which, as their remuneration,
he returned to those who took care
of the land but who never shared
its bounty. In decades a brand
of migrants yearning to be tanned
will swipe it, demand mofongo
from the natives while, like mangos
rotting, their faint feet stain the land.

Nando was born a cane cutter, a machetero. With knife edge he slashed out his own space in the world. His blade greeted stalk like a mother's lips to the back of her baby's knees. He fed the soil with folk tales and cold sweat, and in return it fed his family, dressed his wife, built his home, delivering dignity to his surname. Nando and the cane were simpatico, brothers beyond biology. Hack by chop by chisel his plot grew from one acre to five to one hundred until this concord fed a third of Cabo Rojo.

THE CANE WAS A FOUNTAIN, a church he visited on his day off to thank them for blessing him with sacred azucar. Nando was a machetero, a cane cutter, until the shiny government car arrived with a briefcase full of documents flooded with fine print. The driver of the car told Nando that he came to save him from savagery, he would be liberated from his life of toil, prosperity had finally made its way to the shores of Puerto Rico. Washington had decided the island was to become industrialized. The citizens were told it would provide good jobs for everyone, poverty would be driven from the mountainsides and the shores like fruit flies from the picnic table, and everyone would prosper, everyone except for men like Nando, who was ordered to not grow cane on his land so that the sugar market could be "stabilized."

Nando's beloved cane fields were bullied into barrenness courtesy of the U.S. Department of Agriculture. They promised him he would be paid fairly for faithfully surrendering his talents. Federal subsidies now fed his family, dressed his wife, fixed his house, stripping the dignity from his surname. Nando's three children were packaged and delivered to the factories in the big city, while his other children, the cane, became an echo, AN APPARITION hovering over the hills of his estate that quickly dwindled down from one hundred acres to five to one, where the only cane he now yields is used for the caña that he drinks in his boundless free time, as Nando becomes an orphaned stalk wilting beneath a cataract sun, longing for bygone seasons when things could grow without official permission.

GRITO: AN ALTERNATE HISTORY OF THE PARRANDA

This is how riot becomes love song:
She was the cook. He worked in the fields.

She wanted a garden to play in. He longed
to sauté in her kitchen, offered his chest

for sowing. Both were torched by the touch
of the other. The bane of cédula cleft her

saffron from his sepia, but they would not be
stanched by law scripted in the bottomless

maw of a stranger's patois. At dusk
they charred the finca, kissed to the crackle

of smoldering wheat. The swallowed fumes
became their aphrodisiac. Inebriated

by the embers, they consummated
their marriage with fire, agreed

that they would not stop at their own
bastille. Soon others arrived to witness

the roast. The smoke corralled a swarm
to shadow the couple on their parade

from hacienda to hacienda bearing the gospel
of flame. The burning become their matrimony,

a ceremony held week upon week, where
they turned quintas into cinder, each time

embracing before the glow of the embers,
until time or sea change could halt them.

SUGAR ISLAND FUGUE

Second Voice: 2008

When unions struck down
　　　　nearly every Right-to-work law
the executives were left
　　　　with no scab labor
to exploit in the sweatshops.

They turned to derivatives
　　　　as their mode of plunder,
installing thousands of gigs
　　　　of software from programmers
into their databases.

But they overestimated
　　　　what profit might spring
when they underestimated
　　　　the hacktivists who were
encryption barons of the data cloud.

Their malware devoured the voltaic
　　　　tableau, consuming
every algorithm like a brush fire
　　　　let loose, doing
to the mainframe what the executives

did to artisans. They called
　　　　on their analysts to stop
the speculation, though some thought
　　　　it might have been
the analysts that sent the malware.

The analysts never arrived to help
　　　　extinguish the malware,

because even analysts know there
        is no force that can stop
embittered bytes once they

        catch sight of something sweet.

METASTASIS

. . . And still they came in legions,
platoons of phantasms cloaked in velvet
and steel. They startled us out of our dream
life, gently lulled us into a deeper slumber.
To our simple eyes they were spellbinders,
orators,
magicians who thrust
                    invisible bullets into our
villages. The elders fell like torn
drapery while unnatural light escaped
through the cracks of a glass eye,
pouring shadows into our crock-pots.
The scepter that once stood as our protector
was melted down and made into a satellite
dish.   Lifeless remnants of our children
        were sprinkled onto their ice cream sundaes.
                            Soon on Sundays
we would put our hands together and sing
of borrowed gods, ring bells
                        throughout the valley,
stuffing our secret selves inside
incinerators erected along the dark
alleys that swiftly littered our projects.

Orchestras of insects were flattened,
substituted by a cacophony of metal
horns and electric drills,
                        early morning barrack drills.
Our infinite garden became
        plastic plants set on windowsills.
All the while we sit on front stoops,
unimpressed and unaware,
passing around bottles and cheap
gossip with the smell of sulfur in our hair
until our garments clash with our accents,

                    our heads displaced beneath
                                        train tracks nailed
down across holy ground. We listen to the distractions
refracted from the mouths of manufactured
martyrs,   their tongues serving as the third
rail. Frail and disparate,   we follow
digital red herrings out of our homelands
and into an abyss of disposable
            idols who levy us to witness
                    the impalement of our own myths.

Today we wander along predetermined paths,
            unimpressed and unaware constructing
Byzantine conversations
                    about chimerical enemies
                    and celebrity affairs.
        Transmuted by relentless incantations
        transmitted from an iron
                        tower in the hills,
we whittle away our days scratching
        off incessant lottery tickets,
                            waiting
        for the winning numbers on the radio . . .

THRENODY FOR FREDDIE PRINZE, SR.

Miralo! Check the tint on the box! There's
a glitch stuck in your complexion! A flaquito
Boricua is playing a Mexican! Digame why
the networks can't tell the difference?

While brothers were in the bodeguas kneading
bochinche you cut school to hone your
inflection in hummus flavored hotel lounges.
Where the neighborhood viejitas had lottery

tickets you had punch lines, one liners, chalk
razor lines to part oceans. Hood rats teased
you for taking ballet, but they never been
invited to no L. A. pool party where gringos

chuckled as you paroled their prejudice,
feeding their fetish with fare light enough
for their stomachs, brown tales born light
years from putting greens and ski lodges

of producers and network execs expanding
the distance between you and the projects.
Oye! Jiggle the antenna! There's a clown
prince refugee on prime time! Must have

hopped the 6 train to Mulholland. Red pills
got him seeing stars. Red carpet got him
seeing stars. The agents cut got him seeing
stars. Tu sabes, he got ticketed for being

double consciousness parked on the island
and the sound stage, choking on tour riders,
tabloid photos dropping clues for the coroner,
caught face down in a bathrobe and butterfly

collar of mink draped over the stairway
at the Ritz. Because in those hills they
don't never crown a project Prinze king.
A house is not a novella revising the lives

of the middle aged wives crying at the rich
gringas on the screen because pride won't
let them cry for themselves. You, their well
paid kettle whistle scheming to be first

Hungarican on the moon, news anchors
and casting directors filling your grin
with granite, the applause in the cabaret
making a door prize of your slang. Talk

shows produce tunnel vision, detonating
the bridge to your barrio before the gun
goes off in a premature 3rd act. Your mom
calls you one last time to say she loves

you, but she can't see what you see
when you tell her you been dead a long
time, *mami your project Prinze is gone.*
Freddie's not a man he's a commodity.

Tonight you strut through the pachanga
gigante in the sky, scoping the avenidas
of Washington Heights, seeking the precise
location where you ditched your reflection,

forfeiting your star on the walk of fame,
bitching to management you want
an upgrade from your suite to a brick
flat in The Spanish Harlem of Heaven.

ISLAND: PALENQUES

RICANSTRUCTION: XENOCHRONY

And I caress you with my oceanic hands. And I turn you
around with the tradewinds of my speech. And I lick you with
my seaweed tongues.
And I sail you unfreebootable
                    —Aimé Césaire, *Notebook of a Return to the Native Land*

16. Each time I pass through customs an item is confiscated,
and I am left feeling lighter, heavier. 29. The agent wants
to know my point of origin. I tell him tectonic shifts move
the continents three inches every year, so the only fixed
points are imaginary. 9. And still the mosquitos are quick
to remind us that we are tourists. 18. *Puerto Rico was annexed*
by the United States in 1898 after the Spanish-American
war—the only sentence about the island in my U.S. History
textbook. 31. Mark Lyttle, a Puerto Rican man born in North
Carolina was deported to Mexico. Twice. 4. Eventually you learn
to distrust anything that washes up on the shoreline. 11. Teddy
Roosevelt declared that he would never grant citizenship
to the savages of Puerto Rico unless they agreed to become
civilized and learn English. 21. English is my only language,
a language that has become for me an atoll each time
an aunt tells a joke and I am the only one not laughing,
stranded on a fallow island of monolingualism. 7. In five
decades the moats of the fortress will be refashioned
into casinos. 40. Mother grimaces at the yawling of the rooster.
Abuelo curses the perennial squeals of the subway.
14. To lost jibaros the 6 train sounds like a set of busted
timbales. 25. I am still caged inside the Saturdays of my youth
spent in the rear of my father's Camaro as we sit in traffic
on the George Washington to buy unripe Qenepas from
a graffiti laden Volkswagen van. 33. My wife says the timbales
are punk. She says Hip Hop is punk. Says whenever a world
is built from the trash of conquest it's punk. 10. Then came World
War I. Within months the men were naturalized, given uniforms
and rifles. 30. I have confused a fist for a flag. It was a navigational
error, a collusion of coral and fiberglass. I am the sum total

of history's navigational errors. 1. And my student said to me
I know you ain't Boricua 'cause you speak good. 34. My wife's
professor called us immigrants. 5. In middle school a classmate
asked me if I was going to steal his parent's hubcaps. I asked
him if his parents were going to steal my culture. 12. So long
I've dreamt of stars that I was unaware they glimmered
as buoys along the bay. 8. Passing through customs, I feel lighter,
heavier. 34. It is not enough to have proof of birth in your wallet.
12. Apparently, this is the gringo method for civilizing folks.
35. The agent wants to know if I have any goods to declare.
I tell him that like Sun Ra I wait patiently for the Mother Ship,
convinced the Igneris launched themselves into orbit when
they heard Columbus would be docking on their pier. In my bag,
I tell the agent, I carry the ribs of Betances and a lock
of Blanca Canales' hair. He says these are taxable items.
22. See, the Arawaks and Ostinoids were the first Martians.
19. I'm stretching out to Alpha Centauri, ignoring the bright
and blighted gulleys sparkling beneath my feet. I've fed
unreachable quasars while the gulls on my own shoreline
starve. Had I cooked for just one of them they might have flown
me to my moon of choice. 27. My neighbor thinks the island is a state.
I tergiversate on the futility of plebiscites. 23. My uncles spent three
lifetimes changing light bulbs in the projects so that they might
abscond fom the mainland, never to return. 13. Everyone else but me
seems to have a say about my citizenship. 36. The agent asks how
I identify. I tell him about Jorge Steven Lopez, a transgender
teen who was decapitated 517 years after matriarchy was made
illegal. His head became the star on our flag. His body another
island ardently waiting for sovereignty. 37. I tell him that *I am of no
nationality recognized by the chancelleries*,* I am a liquefied mosaic,
a defamed Orisha biohacked by a French baker and a Galician
aristocrat. 17. I am Rimbaud's oily hair, a curmudgeonly descendant
of the Gauls, a mongrel with a Pentium processor in my skull.
My liver is a Turk, my spleen a Garifuna. 41. My eyes are the Hubble
telescope, my arms the solar panels of the Mir. 2. As a child
I dreamt of being first Sorta Rican on the moon. In middle age

I fantasize about breakdancing across the Neruda crater. Call
me impractical. 19. My Irish grandfather called me a filthy little spic.
He wore thick glasses, could never see the fishing wire that links
the IRA to the FALN. 6. I'll soon become stained glass mounted
in the cathedral of Montserrat, a cracked chalice glued into a Miro
mosaic pedestrians trample upon as they strut across La Rambla.
37. The agent asks me to remove my shoes, wants to know about my accent.
His face winces like the mother of a former flame who told me I was
articulate for a Hispanic. I remind him that 500 years ago he forced me
to put on shoes, now he wants me to take them off again, empty my pockets
and step back through the scanner. I tell him my keys unlock either side
of the coast. The agent says I can take my German uncle on board
with me, but he must confiscate my six nephews from Caguas
and all memory of Rafael Cancel Miranda. The scanner mistakes
my zemí for a bottle of rum. My gills make the agent uneasy.
He says the only fashion accessories permitted on transatlantic
flights are nicotine-blackened lungs, but I left mine on a beach
in Antalya. He says I can keep any cockfights I might have purchased
in the gift shop. The overhead bins are stuffed like fractured oxcarts
hauling unripe yucca. And what island relics are better left behind
at the Terminal Gate? Should I surrender the fried pork, succulent
serial killer of the Antilles? 26. And how many have stopped reading
once they realized I was not speaking of their America? M—
—s will read a book that's one third Elvish, but put two
sentences in Spanish and they think we're taking over.* But I have
read their tomes, read Lovecraft assigning my elders as monstrous
and moulded from some stinking vicious slime of Earth's
corruption, slithering, and oozing . . . in a fashion suggestive of deep
-sea unnamabilities.* 3. My mother dumped a small chemical depot
onto my scalp to keep my hair from protesting the bombings
on Vieques. At the dance the sweat would make toxic molasses
of the gel and singe my cheeks by the third song. 15. A sovereignty
where one third of the population considers abortion to be murder
once conducted force abortions on the island women. Some
of their children were born faceless. I consider myself lucky
to have a face, so I suppose I should not feel slighted. I wish

I could find the head of Jorge Steven Lopez and reattach it to his island
body. 38. The first time I smelled iskender I knew I was home. 32. The parts
of me that slogged through famines outside of Dublin and Civil Wars
in Catalonia become queasy whenever homogenized milk is laid
out on the dinner table. 39. Inside my stomach a fisherman and a scholar
are shipwrecked. They call me to antideluvian streams. 28. I can tell
the Mediterranean is in love with the Caribbean but does not know
how to ask her to go steady. 42. In my bag of contraband I carry the ghost
of Charles Babbage. The wounds of conquest assembled into a Difference
Engine. My spindly fingers are the loom. I juggle with the troubadours
in my own island belly, invite them to a heavy metal parking lot in Perth
Amboy, New Jersey. 24. Indignant and crude, we throw a block party,
wear murals of imprecations as a cumberbund. 43. We syncopate
the roosters and the Hubble, splice qenepas with iskender,
spinning a commonwealth of burnt cane into Godel's theorem,
composing an impossible anthem like a runaway Magritte, blasting
across oceans from ziggurats propped up like amps, a synaesthesia
you can dance to. Each time I pass through customs I feel lighter,

heavier.

*The first asterisked quotation is attributed to Junot Diaz. The other two are cited from Aimé Césaire and H.P. Lovecraft.

SONATA OF THE LUMINOUS LAGOON

after Pedro Pietri

Crickets, coquis corrobórate. Mezzo.
Alto. Tenor. Chemical coladas are pumped

like stale petroleum from fracked rocks.
The joy of combustion at five dollars a pop.

surf shops collide with Desecheo Island.
Silicon Valley Spanish stings like chlorine,

an ill refuge from portfolios and defaulted
mortgages seared on grills that serve no native

dish. The esclavos fed-exed to Co-op city,
Humboldt Park, Kensington, where nature

is a cable program shot from a satellite dish
in twenty minute cycles and sunsets come

with membership fees. Coconuts, cangrejos
are gathered and stacked. For tonight there

will be a fiesta in the hacienda overlooking
Culebra, but the residents did not receive

an invitation. Coral contorts into ads for cell
phones. Panorama in flux. Coffee plantation

permutated into port. Cracked conch serves
as chrysalis for research station. A naval base

etched into islet. Yucca fields tailored into
spa resort. The new natives will boast of job

creation and toast to how the quality of life
has improved for the mosquitos who now

feast on sweet meat of plump and primped
immigrants blown in from el norte.

OXIDATION MURAL OF THE ANTILLES

an island   of
              kerosene   mingling
in the Caribbean
a   red

              jukebox,

    barmaids and teenagers
    sing as
       a giant whale
                                        crashing

              the throat
       of coral

                   this voice   trapped in the

    mango-talk and
                              sad
    st ings   a
         fist

                              old age
    is
                        nothing but music
              hugging
       pauses that live

              luminous   ly. Now
       the needle breathes

    in Spanish

              a trumpet

                    tryin' to cough   up

                            time.
          the chairs   dance

                  and stare,
               the water
    sings   *a wave*
For the hens, now

           the hurricane   brewing   Barbados
               will be
            fishing

                      in every yard

         ,   sleeping   , the names   gone dark
will   be   teasing
   a   mouth   believing
      the end of   island   life has been
scribbled on   song.

Erasure of "Hugging The Jukebox" by Naomi Shihab Nye

OPERATION SERENITY (CENTER PANEL)

Six miles separate you from the tower of Yuisa.   Your skin is wrapped in sea salt and
sarcasm.   Last month four tourists died here when they decided to not follow the trails or
read the park signs. Park rangers spent nine days searching for them. You have no trouble
reading signs,   even when you don't like what they are telling you. You wore the wrong

kind of shoes for all this, and you've got a wedding to attend this evening, but your friend's
father has been swallowed by a staph infection like plankton between whale teeth. Three miles
separate you from the tower of Yuisa.   The coast bulges like a Botero. Your trail is a sliver
of licorice. Last month four tourists died here among the False Birds of Paradise. They decided

maps are for those who believe in returning.   They were lost like their elders but lacked
the talons to cut their way back to their point of origin. Where they veered you shed your
veneer and you climb.   You climb to find the accent your mother buried in 1973. You
climb thinking you might be able to shed the part of you that throbs in the presence of others.

There is a wedding this evening but the screech owl has led you to falls you won't find in
Newark.   You strip to rinse yourself in the shallow end. The falls drown your eyes until
they mistake the forest for a mural spotted on Jacinto Street. Inside the tower of Yuisa
you can see the tides that pulled in diseased galleons five hundred years ago. The clouds

straggle across Kandinsky hills. Here you promise to find the courage to give all that was
exported from your island like coffee tins.   Last month four tourists died here because they
had trouble staying inside the lines.   The caciques would have escorted them to the stars and
back again, but the first time they played docent the tourists muzzled them for eternity.

You won't relearn the language that was stolen from you, but you will come to invent your
own.   You will teach it to your students, and you will build a library with your beloved.
The libraries of this cay have been reduced to rubble,   but every plate of yucca with garlic
passed around the patio sings like the satellite of Arecibo emitting low frequency flirtations

> across the heavens. Yocahu and Atabey
> emerge from the haze to deliver you
> gently back to the foot of El Yunque. Six
> miles separate you from the Tower of Yuisa.

DÉCIMARINA

Guaorabo River, 1511

Salcedo desired four guides
from Urayoan to deliver
him unsoaked across the river
Guaorabo, as if one could ride
a man like a horse, as if tides
could be bullied. The four men hauled
Salcedo halfway until they
were stricken with the urge to test
the Spaniard's presumed deathlessness.
They submerged him until nightfall,

doggedly holding him to the floor
of the riverbed to be sure
his spirit no longer endured.
Once they were convinced their captors
were mortals the four went before
Urayoan to share the news.
Caciques convened. The ruse
was dispelled, the driven mule kicked,
the cay shook as they raised the wick
of rebellion and lit the fuse.

VOX POPULI FOR THE MAROONED

After Julia De Burgos and Mahmoud Darwish

Like a charm of goldfinches we will gather. We will gather at the sea
crest and inside toppled cubicles, drawing upon this horizon of shady
treaties and chemical weapons depots as if cajoled toward the coast

by the sheen of a lighthouse. We will gather upon the terraces
of a crumbling metropolis and along the dunes of Atacama, Mojave,
Kalahari. We will gather like tectonic tremors echoing in the caterwauls

of beggars in Fresno and cancer stricken housewives in Beijing, quantize
this throng of lamentations into a rumba. Shirking the title of rabble,
we will gather the rubble from the sewer grates and flooded cellars
of Palestine and Fukushima, of Detroit and La Paz, and we will tether

the scintilla of plywood and plastic into a hope shrouded oasis. We will
gather not like mold or like flies, but like tidal waves or skate punks
darksliding the rim of a jilted pool. We will gather to consider how

the scent of baked bread can travel effortlessly across epochs when no
barricades are raised along fairways and boulevards. We will gather
beckoned by a mammoth hunger. We will share blankets and soup

with our enemies, and we will remind the unwitting that all are deserving
of honey and soap. We will carve up this night with candles and canticles.
The splintering of our tibias will spark the lovelorn to squawk. We will

gather like pigeons on dead phone lines. We will be a bog of gleaming
skin skimming through blizzards promulgating a terminal armistice.
We will gather in Selma and Port-Au-Prince, in Monrovia and Manila.

We will break nothing when we leave, bind ourselves like cloth around
a fevered chest, float across plazas like a warm sponge over a sore shin,
and become a shameless shore of sin carousing, a flesh tinted mandala

of static bribing the sky with the promise that we will gather here each
day until fear is in need of hospice. And we will come bearing incense
and peach pie and whenever the wounds of injustice are salted in our

favelas we will gather again in the squares of Tianemen and Taksim, of Tahrir and Trafalgar, of Bolivar and Union. Like barnacles or fluorescent algae, we will gather . . . we will gather . . . we will gather . . .

BRICOLAGE:

Greasy surrogate cannibal.
Overeducated Caliban.
Caribbean Taliban.

Chop shop of hypodermic
platanos, switchblades,
black beans and boleros.

Island cabaña boy toy.
Man maid. Tantric tour
guide. Hip shaking simian.

Ghetto clown. Bare
back bar back in braids.
Café y pan handler.

Bragadocious
Ostinerd
in ostinato.

Housebroken ethnic
token. Street cred
legitimizer. Case study.

Test subject. Abject object
of hostility. Fertility charm.
Strutting sancocho

of styles. Hopping
the Antilles like
Cleopatra rode the Nile.

ARCHIPELAGO:

neither boundary
            nor center
neither master nor serf

this breadth of hillside
and coast
            is kaleidoscope
beyond imprisonment
            or liberty

jumbled pollen
of *finca*   and barrio
plantation   penitentiary
            play ground

            tidal waves
stanch the stench wafting
from the machine
                        of spume

the caravel that carries
the nightmare
            to the sleeper

criollo   and coolie
emerge from the silt
like smelted treasure
copper rhythm seeps
            into plumbing

the flota arrives
            splicing the reefs
the ports
            are abandoned

EIDOLONS:

        Recast Hostos
as rogue web journalist
        taking on
corporate crime
        Recast Toussaint
as house DJ moonlighting
as civil rights lawyer
Recast Agueynaba
            as South Bronx
            social worker
Recast Guaman Poma
as union leader of migrant
farmers   Recast
Metacom as queer rapper
            with major label
distribution
Recast Zumbi as tattooed
holistic healer
from Bushwick
            Recast Sor Juana
as front woman
in a straight edge
punk band   Recast
Coatlicue as Mumbai
bond slave burning her
sari   Recast Yuisa
as a goth girl with a Ph.D.
            in Physics
            Recast Manco
Inca as graffiti
writer who mentors
incarcerated youth
Recast Sandino
as ace pitcher who builds
schools   for the poor

Atabey returns
            to give her
two weeks notice.

Recast Manuela Sanz
            as talk show host
possessing
a bottomless charity fund.

MOSAIC: ZEMÍS

HELIOTROPIC CRAB CANON

Icarus as Felix Baumgartner

        Blooming from dark matter,
I burst.
        Then like a nova
cleaving eternity
        I vault
    through the tropopause
demanding an answer
        from immortals.
    Gallant taunts,
love notes
      advance like
The planets
   of the hungry.
They lack the will
   to catch me.
    Clouds refuse
the impossible,
    prodding me toward
a stilted desire.
    This ghostly ceiling
        rupturing
    my will
becomes the meridian,
    beliefs
   as fragile as
     breath.
      Conceit incites angst
   with a lone touch,
this sky
    electrifying
a winged eel
     that spirals like
a soft comet
   in a space suit.

Icarus as Agüeybaná the Brave

Splintered
   from Earth
like an egg shell
   dripping,
ground
   becomes
  my belly
emptied, punctured
    like ozone,
   like a syringe
  piercing the epidermis.
I am an arrow tail
   in a space suit,
  a soft comet
    that spirals like
a winged eel
   electrifying
this sky
   with a lone touch.
      Conceit incites angst.
   Breath
as fragile as
  beliefs
becomes the meridian,
   my will
    rupturing
this ghostly ceiling,
a stilted desire
   prodding me toward
the impossible.
   Clouds refuse
to catch me.
They lack the will
   of the hungry.

I am an arrow tail
      piercing the epidermis
          like a syringe,
              like ozone.
Emptied. Punctured.
      My belly
          becomes
ground
      dripping
like an egg shell
          from Earth,
splintered.

The planets
          advance like
love notes,
                gallant taunts
      from immortals
demanding an answer.
          Through the tropopause
              I vault,
cleaving eternity.
              Then like a nova
I burst,
              blooming dark matter.

SORTA RICAN BOOK OF DREAM (A BRIDGE VERSION)

Quicksand

1. Sinking in quicksand that smells like burnt cauliflower
   means that on your wedding night the photographer
   will forget to remove his lens cap while capturing the kiss.

Rooms

1. Painted to resemble a city beach means that you will
   get a big promotion for a job that doesn't pay you.
2. With the furniture on the ceiling means that you will
   receive an honorary degree for your research
   on the sleeping patterns of superstar DJ's.
3. A classroom the size of a football field (known by most
   gringos as a soccer field) where the school janitor
   makes fun of you means that you will win an all-
   expenses-paid vacation to Tucumcari, New Mexico.

Squirrel

1. A squirrel carrying a balloon with the face of Emma
   Goldman on it means that a calamity of bow ties
   will be left in your glove box the evening after next.

Water

1. A glass of water means you want to quit your job
   to become a licensed figment of the imagination.
2. A muddy pond means you want to quit your job
   to become a licensed figment of the imagination.
3. An ocean means you want to quit your job
   to become a licensed figment of the imagination.
4. A plastic pool means you want to quit your job
   to become a licensed figment of the imagination.
5. A single teardrop means you want to quit your job
   to become a licensed figment of the imagination

PORTRAIT OF IRIS MORALES
AT THE YOUNG LORDS OFFICES, SEPTEMBER 1970

You might want to deign those rosy cheeks
    nectarous because you mistake them

for wax angels mounted in your cathedrals
    of guilt. But those cheeks were forged

from the scabrous ruins left by San Ciriaco.
    She is not yet old enough to vote, but she

knows that when men speak of progress
    what follows is a steel cut anemia

that creeps into the floorboards like water bugs
    the super will never come to exterminate.

Her contraposto posture is pure contraband,
    a reclamation project of lashes

that remember the overseer's lash. Each
    holstered fist awaits ascension

as she commands an arc of stars freshly
    emancipated from their flag.

Hidden are her teeth that do not smile
    on command, teeth carved from the cay

where Atabey gave birth to the Caribbean
    Sea. Such royalty is unfit for a low income

tenement. She's caught wind that the Grand
    Concourse is merely a doppelgänger

of the Middle Passage. Her hips are not child
            bearing hips. They are factory strike

inciting hips. Hips that raise consciousness,
            not infants. Best believe she did not come

to this peninsula looking for a government
            check. She came to build a rainforest

upon this gully of busted radiators, to send the cat
            callers and councilmen scampering.

Ekphrastic of a photo from "Pa Lante!" taken by Michael Abramson

CREPUSCULE WITH GRISEL

panting. sighing. an ankle angled over a thigh. you blush.　　a rush. lips spread like wings
of a pigeon. skin harvested. fields plowed.　　a partly cloudy afternoon. a disrobing.
an uneasy feeling. an unexpected heat. sweat beads like prayer beads. an imperfect curvature.
a voluptuous wall. a matchstick's red head rubbed on flint. an intent gaze. unattached. a nose
entrenched in a chin. lotion applied to a calf.　　a calf slaughtered
for the feast. a secret drawn in a fleshy fold. a promise unattached. a wrist rotated
counterclockwise. a quivering. a trinket falls to the fall. two bells conjugated like a verb. your
mercurial poise.　a feline pose.　lock and key joined.　　an unhinged door opened twice.
oasis. water lapped by a newt's tongue. silent rhythm. a heartbeat out of synch.
an eyelash sculpture like a lone peacock. four legs woven into a wicker basket.　sliding.
ungraceful pirouettes. buttons sewn onto a turquoise vest.　clipped nails and clipped beaks.
concurrent currents of parallel streams. a distant pulse. stifled polemics.　breathe from a laugh,
resurrected. your cheeks, pillows. a sliding door. a cracked inkwell. a cupped hand mistaken
for as a safety net. a fumbling. a rescinding. a receding.

　　a whisper.
　　a squeeze.
　　a trembling.

a treble clef. a cleft heart, unattached. a broken circle. a mountain interrupted
by a valley.　attached. unattached. attached. unattached. an attaché case stuff with ripe plums.
a scent ascending. a symphonic moaning. a phone disconnected. a flexion. affliction. a tension.
extension. torque and sweet thunder. a clenched fist. a bit lip. candle wax on a dead victrola.
a flood. a flushing. a draught. an opening.　　a closing unrelated. cracked eggs on a kitchen floor.
a well times seizure. a departure. the singed cuff of a smoking jacket. two car radios playing the
same station. a refraction.
an unfurling. an unmasking. a question left unasked. a contraction. a contradiction.
an unveiling. a cleansing. a becoming. a breath, unattached. a death, unattached.
a thumbprint on a pelvis. a promise, unattached. a bosom, unattached. a diamond heist
hatched. a grape pluck. an orange, peeled. a puddle in the driveway. a pillow wrung.
unattached. a fugue hummed. a trail of pink silt. unattached. a torpor. a pelt. a moth and
a flask. a singing matroshka. a riddle planted in a blue belly. a summons. a murmur.
a bewilderness. a plate of dried figs. a lost earring. an ebbing. an echo. a trembling.

　　An oil painting
　　In the den
　　Waiting to be hung.

THRENODY FOR JEAN-MICHEL BASQUIAT

comes the point the splicing
       of rubber teeth with polymer kings
    becomes chiasma   becomes collision of ink
and light
so bright you got to gaze
    into the phrase
'till that splash of black beige   summons 20/20 blindness
    ~~to uplift the tatted congregation~~

          comes the point the blushing
            of the dustheads ~~the erudite~~
    ~~vulgarity~~   of copyrighted deities
snaps   like subtitles ~~tran~~scribing
this Boom For Real   like a spit-shined amen
    comes the point

    the work just stinks of WOW
  each fleck   ~~and shake~~   of brush baked
  with glint   ~~of howWHYwhatwhat~~
    where the geography
  scrolled out   inside the skull
    is more expansive than the low
  rent studio where it sleeps
    Comes the point   where what

is scratched   on plaster in blood
   orange wafts like onion gum
    where wicker wings can't
 hold optic nerves can't hold
 the ~~ob~~noxious   fumes where yellow oil cans can't
   spill quickly enough
   to prevent asbestos and niacin
from gentrifying   flipped medullas   soon

 the self portrait   is a landscape ~~of whyHOWwhat~~
  soon comes the point where   the mask

becomes more real than the face
where irradiated fortunes glisten
bent in blotted
blue   chasms of ~~pocked~~ pollinated phrenia where
the neoteny of sly primates
conceals confabulations
of the fashion   mongers   among us   comes

the point   how sausage fame ~~oxidi~~zes
the lathe   of ~~corpus~~ corpses callosums collapse
                   and the room stinks of WOW &
the reverb   you see can't be miss taken
                   for an other
                   ~~wherewhen~~why the color of this cosmology
                   is shipped to the fat farm   to shed
~~the chromatic~~   ~~singularity~~   ~~of zulu and zeus~~

                              comes the joint
                              why the magic of the marker
                                        is conflated
                                        as ~~unadulterated~~
                   ~~anger comes~~ &

          the suture   ruptures
          the point
          the paint thrashes
          the curators   lips where xenochrony
                               of mauve and alabaster
                               just stinks of wow &
          the dearly   deep arted peel off
          the walls   to confound the flatlanders
                               looking for a sound ~~in~~vestment &
          the same ol'

samo hangs the ol' shames out to dry and rot and reek
                    ~~like cankers~~ like

                                        a gri-gris
                                        to ward

off sham
reflections

with this boom this
for this real this rock
this wow this pop
this why this
what this
stinks this

TROPICODEX

seeking a vanishing point with an unobstructed vista

you erect a pier of turtle shells and lizard feet

stretching across the Atlantic

cast fishing lines into a pool of fiberglass and unfiltered water

you erect a pier hoping to catch the last grouper

a pier that peers into bays

where skeletons of doubt check into shabby hostels

with a view of dead ceremonies

your pier spans the distance of *the gulf of unwanted testimonies*

a pier that leaves your peers questioning

your sanity like you question their motives

seeking a vanishing point you dig

for wooden keys beneath palm leaves

and thatched rum shacks

keys to a pier where the horizon stuns

the coin collectors into a blue torpor

thirsty and mystified   you erect a pier without end

on a cape where sea urchins and jibaros

curl into a single

silver wave

Wayna Capac: A Parable Remixed

after Eduardo Galeano

No slave had toiled as ardently as Wayna
Capac. He pulled more gold from the mines
than 100 men. Wayna Capac was so efficient

that he was invited to dine with the overseers,
though he politely declined, said he had
no time to waste, there was still gold

to be rousted out of its pitch black
slumber. They were so proud of their
little workhorse that they did not expect

to wake up to find their spoils had
disappeared and their galleon set out
to sea without them aboard. When they

pried the men about who would commit
such a crime, Wayna Capac politely stood up
to take the credit, saying to them,

Your precious gold is on your ship. You better go catch it.
We do not want the gold here for it is a curse. It has brought
us the worst kind of pestilence. It brought us you.

Tergiversatyrs

after The Mars Volta

Somnambulant I saunter
through ziggurats of din.

        My hallowed predilections
ricochet incongruently,   a daft sacrilege

of corpuscles swelling. I gutted a matroshka
vacillating between bohíos and megalopolis.

The debilitated slanderer applied sibilant
tourniquets to my lacerated testaments.

Goat hoofed czars remand these shivering
       asphodels,   a levy inflicted

as penance for my recalcitrant marrow.
        The cybernetic scarab

fashions an amulet out   of insouciant
scabs while   your copper tongued

magistrate commits sepulcher sermons.
Wistful conclaves ululate in their brigs.

I palaver with cadavers.   My bludgeoned
mission ossifies vicariously, consummating

with emaciated ornaments, an inoculation
of subterfuge   to my phantom spine.

Circulus

after Chick Corea and Paco De Lucia

from the seventh galaxy   a yellow nimbus,
city of brass   in crystal silence.

                        parallelogram shaped
        heart.   yamaha in heat.
      ruby swan child crooning
          a spastic waltz.

     marmoreal seraphs sundered
               from billowing
   arpeggios.   sierra of languor.
   pliant and sloping.

city of brass   from the seventh galaxy
in crystal silence.   a yellow nimbus.

                   sybilant paradise.
             somnambulent forever.
       jester   and tyrant duel when
      sunday's duende swoons.

     brash underbrush of spotted
           bright.   besotted sorceress.
  discombobulated herons.   crescent
        carnival of prayer.

a yellow nimbus   in a city of brass.
from crystal silence   the seventh galaxy.

Hunt's Point Kwansaba

after The Last Poets

Head phone mecca, gym shoe palace, annex

of the *kapali carsi*, your dollar stores

wed the Yangtze to the Orinoco, your

curb doubles as a pulpit, the smell

of incense and jerk chicken blesses every

night shift toiler and bionic mom, your

docks feed the flocks in every borough.

GUANÍN

This island like a basket
of laundry accidentally
bleached. This island
of moon shine and conch
shells, of open air bars with
signs above the register
that read *All discussion
of politics is strictly
forbidden*. This island,
a naval outpost, a mouth
of grinding teeth, a daft
protégé, a promenade
princess, a receptacle
for spectacle, a marvel
of glistening skin. This island
like a hen house above
the garage, cocks heckling
the dawn. This island like
a deflated basketball
or a bag of yucca falling
off the delivery truck.
This island that eludes
you like your first crush
in a game of freeze tag.
This island is a bridge
between the Orishas
and the astronauts.
This island is a blender,
polychrome vortex stirring
the soot of the empire
with *abrazos* and *batas*.

ABOUT THE AUTHOR

VINCENT TORO is a poet and playwright from New York, where he teaches for The City University of New York's Bronx Community College and The Dream Project, a non-profit organization that places working artists in the schools and local communities. He has an MFA from Rutgers University, received a 2014 Poet's House Emerging Poet's Fellowship, and was awarded a New York Foundation for the Arts Fellowship in Poetry for 2014. His poems have been published in *Rattapallax, The Paterson Literary Review, Vallum, Bordersenses, Kweli Literary Journal, The Buenos Aires Review, Really System, Five Quarterly, Codex, Duende Literary Journal,* and in the anthologies *CHORUS,* edited by Saul Williams, and *The Waiting Room Reader 2,* edited by Rachel Hadas.

AHSAHTA PRESS

NEW SERIES

AHSAHTA PRESS

SAWTOOTH POETRY PRIZE SERIES

This book is set in Apollo MT type and Frutiger
with Bauer Bodoni titles
by Ahsahta Press at Boise State University.
Cover design by Quemadura.
Book design by Janet Holmes.

AHSAHTA PRESS
2016

JANET HOLMES, DIRECTOR

ASHLEY BARR
DENISE BICKFORD
PATRICIA BOWEN, *intern*
KATIE FULLER
ZEKE HUDSON
COLIN JOHNSON
INDRANI SENGUPTA